WEEDING OUT THE RIFFRAFF

In Pursuit of My Spiritual Journey

LESLIE GREEN

This is an autobiography of the author's life experiences. However, some names and situations are fictional.

Books written by the author

Hi Mom, It's Me
Thanks for Being My DAD
Available from Amazon.com

I Can Only Be Me
Available from pocpacs@yahoo.com

Table of Contents

Introduction   vii
Acknowledgments   ix

Chapter 1   The Stage Is Set   1
Chapter 2   The Shallow Road   8
Chapter 3   Step Lightly   14
Chapter 4   Fall and Burn   19
Chapter 5   Open Your Eyes, Fool   46
Chapter 6   Listen Carefully   51
Chapter 7   Take These Chains off of Me   59
Chapter 8   Unravel My Soul   74
Chapter 9   Speak to Me, Lord!   81
Chapter 10   Distractions in Pursuit of
             My Spiritual Journey   100
Chapter 11   God's Grace   109

Summary   119
A Note from the Editor   121

Introduction

When we come into this world, we come to believe that it is going to be a wonderful place that we can enter. Little did I know that I had to weed out the riffraff to get to the marvelous, the magnificent and most enlightening spiritual journey of my life.

Acknowledgments

This book is dedicated to my family. My children: Anika Simone Johnson, my only smart, lovely, and beautiful daughter; my second-born, my son, Kashif Hassan Green, who has finally embraced life and is working on what is pleasing in the sight of God; and my youngest son, Dennis Saeed Nimmons, my intelligent, wildest child, who has had a hard time fully understanding the great wealth he possesses within himself—being a vessel for the Almighty God. I need to say that being your mother has been and continues to be a great, challenging, and enlightening journey. I pray daily that all of you reach beyond your present situations and follow the walk that I've led you toward, which is to love the Lord God with all your heart, mind, and soul. He is the only one who can make or break you, so don't ever give the power to people, places, or things because they are insignificant when it comes to Lord Jesus.

My second dedication goes to my Bishop of Upper Room Full Gospel Baptist Church in Brooklyn, New York: Bishop William G. Bennett, Pastor and Overseer. You probably don't know this but you changed my life. I remember moving away from Bedford Stuyvesant (Bed-Stuy) and trying to find a church closer to home. I had a hard time balancing worship, prayer, and work. I remember coming back and forth to church, and at that time you would prophesy to me. I knew that you had to be a vessel for the Lord because how could you tell me intimate details of my life if God wasn't with you and operating through you? I've gained much respect and admiration for you—being young and able to give your life to the Almighty God. Over the years, I watched people coming and going and could not understand some of the things that were happening. However, now I do. You are doing exactly what the Lord commissioned us to do: sending out disciples to carry the good news into the world. If I had not walked into Upper Room many years ago, I do not know where would I be! Thank you, Bishop Bennett, for listening to me and understanding my cry. I am a changed, mature, and grateful woman. For that, I truly appreciate you. I pray daily for you and your family, and I believe God will continue to bless you beyond measure.

My next dedication is to Mr. Lemuel Mials, who was Center Manager at Von King Cultural Center in Brooklyn, NY. God bless you! When I arrived at the center and asked for assistance in 2002, you were so kind and loving to me. You had no idea how damaged I was due to the bad experiences I had had with men. At that time, the last thing I wanted was to be led by a man. I believe God led me to you as a part of my healing process. For that, I am truly grateful. Because of your genuine humanitarian spirit, I've been able to look at men in a brighter light. You helped me get more courage and opened my eyes to a brand new me. Don't get me wrong; even at sixty, I'm still learning. You helped me present my first live theatre production, and I know it was only possible because of the grace of God and the wisdom he has bestowed upon you. I always pray that God keeps you and provides for you and your family with the greatest gifts in life. God has truly laid his hand upon you. God bless you, Mr. Mials. To God be the Glory. My next dedication is to my church family, Upper Room Baptist Church. Wow, where am I to start? I'm not going to list all of the names of my church brothers and sisters because the list is too long. However, as you read this, you will know who you are. I need to say thank you, thank you, and thank you. You all have been more of a family to me, good, bad, and indifferent. Everyone has made an impact in molding my wonderful and blessed life. I pray God blesses each and every one of you and gives to you all that your hearts desire. May God continue to bless you all in a mighty way.

My last but surely not least dedication is to my close friends. I refuse to name any of you because it may cause conflict. However, when you read my book, you will know who you are. To my special friends, thank you for listening to my crazy ideas, my hurts, my opinions, my dreams, and my aspirations. Sometimes I repeated myself over and over, but you always listened. You have no idea that if it weren't for you, I would have lost my mind. I pray that God gives all of you what your hearts desire. You mean so much to me. Remember to praise the Lord and keep God first.

CHAPTER 1

The Stage Is Set

Most people don't realize that children can hear from inside the womb. The womb to me was dark and warm, and safe from external stimuli. As far as I remember, I heard a conversation between my biological parents, which I found to be a negative one. I can remember my father saying in a harsh voice: "What are you talking about? You're pregnant? You know I'm married." They were arguing in loud voices. Immediately I thought to myself: "I don't like him." I don't know how many months old I was then, but I must have been developed enough to hear clearly. I decided that I was going to make his life a living hell. Huh, his life a living hell? Little did I know that when I came out, I'd embark on a journey that would make my life a living hell, until the spirit of the Living God would manifest himself in me.

That was the first thing I remember. The second thing I remember was being three years old, sitting on this huge, fluffy couch. That couch was so comfortable I still remember it today. It seemed like such a happy time. I cannot remember being one or two years old, but at three years of age, we had a lot of music, and family and friends came to visit often. Most of my family members were artistic. If they couldn't sing (singing that sounded like angels from heaven to me), they played a musical instrument.

I remember getting goosebumps when I heard them sing or play music. They sang songs that were sung during the time when Billie Holiday was around. Billie Holiday: the songstress with the sultry voice that would make men melts in their seats. They used to say, "Billie Holiday use to sing at the bar on Bedford Avenue and Dean Street at the corner of our block." My mother and father would go down there to escape the realities of their world, just for a moment or two.

They knew this guy named Lewis who worked at the club. He would come back with them and a couple of the other musicians as well.

Then, we had what they called "jam sessions" back then, in our huge living quarters. Our living room was so big that you could have turned it into a club. I don't know what kind of apartments they're making now, but our living room was humongous. That's probably why I need to have a lot of space even today. This experience impacted my life. The most euphoric feelings I have, come from entertainment. From that time on, I enjoyed live shows. That was when the "stage of my life was set." Living in the late fifties and early sixties was confusing and scary but also involved happy times. Little did I know what had happened earlier would shape my life for the future and set the stage as well. As a young girl growing up in that era, I was trained to observe and not speak, to be seen and not heard—or if you want to put it bluntly, to shut my mouth and mind my own business. Keep what happens here; leave it here where it belongs. Therefore, later in life, my communication skills were poor, until… I'll explain later. At times, my life seemed normal and happy, until the arguments and physical abuse began. I found out later that my father, although married to someone else, was abusive and a heroin addict. My father disappeared at times—where I don't know. I found out later that he had gone to jail. Quiet as it was kept, I was glad. I felt more secure and stable when he wasn't there. My mother decided to let some family members stay with us. At first, I did not mind, but when my aunt talked to me, she scared me. I felt neglected. Although I loved my aunt, she had two little babies and everyone catered to them. So I withdrew within myself. My mother had one boyfriend whom I really liked. His name was Lewis; he was six-feet tall, light-skinned, well fit and fine. He was the sweetest male figure I'd ever met. He was a service man, kind, gentle, and always willing to help. I don't know what happened to him up until today. I think he was killed in the war, but it's vague to me. All my life, I have wished my mother had married him, but guess what, she never married. She continued to have relationship after relationship with my father, the jailbird, and other men throughout her life.

My world felt like a rollercoaster ride. Even today, I don't like those rides. My immediate family, my older sister, resented me. We were four years apart. I do not like to bring this up—but, you know the dark and light skin thing? Well, I am here to tell you it does exist. I was light, and she was dark. For some reason, she would pick on me until my little brother was born. Up until the day she left this earth, she held this resentment toward me. God rest her soul. Let me continue. She used to tell me to do things to my brother that would make him cry. I would, but I would be sad and scared because if I didn't do it, she would hurt me. I finally got up the nerve one day, at the age of five, to tell her that I wasn't going to hurt my little brother anymore because I liked him. She said: "I like him too." So we began taking good care of him. I was happy and felt good that I had stood up for myself. This too was a part of the stage that was set up for me.

All my life I would allow myself to do things that were uncomfortable to please others until it was unbearable. People pleasing is very un-healthy. At a very young age, I learned a lot of unhealthy and life-threatening behaviors that could have and would have taken me out of this earthly realm. But with the Grace and Mercy of God, I am still here and traveling on a road that has proven to become what you would call a "spiritual journey."

Growing up for me became a chore and not a wonderful experience—so I thought. Although I had many trials and tribulations, and some tragedies, I continued to have faith and truly believed that there was a power greater than myself. I know now that all of those situations and experiences molded me into this wonderful, mature, and caring individual I am today. Don't get me wrong; I still have work to do, people to see, places to go, and messages to be revealed. No, I have not arrived. When I get to that point, I guess I'll be going home to be with the Father.

CHAPTER 2

The Shallow Road

The road that I landed made me aware of my sexuality. Remember, I told you there were a lot of people in my house? Well, they were having sexual relations till the wee hours of the morning. Even way back then I would be awake and having trouble sleeping, but I could not understand what was happening to me. Talk about living life on the edge. I could feel my body reacting and did not understand why. People don't realize that, at a young age, a child can become sexually aroused. This opened up my sexual appetite. I began to go on the prowl and find little boys at age five who would allow me to entice them, and who eventually got tired of me bothering them. It wasn't fun; it was sick. But guess what? In some ways, it was healthy at the same time. We are equipped like that. I cannot tell you when I stopped, but eventually I did, for a little while … All of these experiences molded me and took from me at the same time. I remember starting school and I hated it—absolutely hated it. I do not know when and where it started, but I thought I was a princess and that I should be catered to. Where did it come from? I could kind of give you an idea … I discovered that the door was opened by my sister. Remember I told you that she didn't like me. She also would tell me, "You think you are better than anyone else." I had gotten tired of her telling me that, so I took on the role. What a way to reject something but to become that very thing! Later in life, I had to relearn behaviors that would benefit me and get rid of the ones that were hurting me. Not an easy task, but doable. Well, as time went on, I remember some of my years in school and others I would rather forget. After coming to the conclusion that I hated school, the next thing I remember is that we moved quite often. This made it hard to keep friends or establish friendships.

I felt displaced from birth until I was thirteen years old, which is when I established my own roots. But before I go there, let me backtrack and elaborate about this school thing and some even more pertinent events that shaped my personality. The next school grade I recall is fourth grade. I finally felt a sense of belonging. It was a laidback year. Our block, Pacific Street between Bedford and Franklin Avenue, became a play street during the summer. What that means is that the street was blocked off for the whole summer. We could play in the street for the entire day without worrying about getting hit by a car. It was nice. We also were honored with service men (army) that summer. On Pacific Street and Bedford Avenue is an armory. That is where the service men stayed when they came home. It is still there to this day but is now a men's shelter. When I was nine, there was one service man I had a crush on. I am now grateful he was a gentleman. He never disrespected me or even got fresh, as some older men did later in my life—men who are now called pedophiles. That summer I had a great time for the most part. I also had a best friend; her name was Savannah. I thought that was the prettiest name I'd ever heard. She lived in the biggest house on our block. It was so huge, it had two sides to it. We used to roam around the house and look for things to get into. One day, Savannah said: "I have to show you something." I said: "What is it?" We went up on one side of the house and looked through the peek holes and saw couples having sex. What a turn on and off that was! Anyway, when we got a chance we did that quite often, until it got stale. Well, as life would have it, a new boy moved in the neighborhood. He was so cute! His name was Michael. He was light-skinned with curly hair and gorgeous gray eyes. He was soft-spoken and friendly. Savannah and I took him hostage. We kept him with us all the time. I felt like I had a boyfriend and a girl-friend, and I liked them both very much. One day, the three of us were together, and he said, "Let me see you and Savannah kiss." So we did. He couldn't make up his mind as to which of us he wanted to be with, so we took turns kissing him. Well, after a while, I got offended and decided that I did not like this. I told myself that I liked him and her, and I just wanted to be friends with both of them. I said to them, "If you want to be boyfriend and girlfriend, go ahead." I did not want to share. So I only got with them to play child-like games, and that was that. I discovered something about myself: I needed a lot of different stimuli or I would get bored. I started hanging out with this girl in my building. She was a thief and liked living on the edge. I thought it might be fun until … we got caught. It was not nice and I got my first lesson in how your "so-called friends will turn their back on you." She took me to the corner store and told me to put the candy in my pocket, and I did. We got caught and were scolded. So she decided to get money out her mother's piggybank. Her mother was sleeping because she was a drunk. People would tease my friend about her mom, and I felt sorry for her. Although my own home situation was not that great, I had empathy even at that age. I was also a people pleaser, remember? Anyway, we began to climb into her apartment from the back window because they lived on the first floor. I asked her, "Why are we doing this?" She replied, "It is fun." So I went with it. Although I began to feel uncomfortable about doing it, I continued. We kept doing it until all of the money was gone out of the piggybank. After it was over, I felt guilty. We lived on the fourth floor. So later that evening, her mother knocked on our door. I became really uncomfortable. My mother went into the hallway to talk to her, and then called me out there and asked what had happened. I told my mother the truth. She offered to pay my friend's mother back. I told my mother it was my friend's idea. That became my first lesson of defining a "so-called friend" and how you can't trust them. That experience set the stage for yet another unhealthy relationship and also prompted me to step lightly. It got worse before it got better.

CHAPTER 3

Step Lightly

As time went on and due to the previous experiences I'd had, I began to be very cautious about most of the things I got into. When I was ten, we moved again. That year was full of overwhelming changes, disappointments, and encounters that would shatter my life forever. Since we'd had moved again, I had no friends, and the new neighborhood kids were sizing me up. We lived in a building that housed mostly girls. You would think that would be fun, but it wasn't. The tenement was infested with mice and roaches. My father was with us again, arguing with my mom as usual. We were often low on food, and I remember being hungry. I could not understand why on God's earth my mother continued to keep this man around who wasn't a good provider. I hated him with a passion. I'd promised myself that I would never get involved with a man like that! For the most part, I didn't but I got involved with the emotionally unavailable ones. Anyway, the girls on the second floor liked to pick on people and as time went on, I ended up getting into a fight with one of the younger sisters. It's funny; after all the dust had settled, we became friends.

There were also three sisters who lived next door to us. They got punished often. Their mother would make them stand in the hallway and hold up one of their legs. I felt so sorry for them. I would sit in the back room and open our back door to talk to them. Our tenement was a railroad flat. That's an apartment-type complex with the rooms in a straight line. One day, the older sister told me how we could get some candy money. I remember asking, "From where?" Little did I know that her mother used to have different "male company," if you know what I mean…

Anyway, she told me that we had to do something to get our candy money. When I asked

"What?" she said that the exterminator would give us money. This exterminator had a store-front. She said, "We would have to step lightly in the back of the building, without getting caught." I asked her, "What do we have to do?" She said, "We have to lie on top of him and let him hump on us and he'll give us .50." I said, "Oh, I could do that." Now mind you, we were eleven, ten, nine years old, and her little sister was five… I could see how sick in the head this man was. He was an older Jewish man between thirty and fifty years old. I was appalled that he also did this to her five-year-old sister.

My mind told me that he had to pay, so I took a chance and went in there by myself, to see how far he would go. Very dangerous! I could have lost my life, but I did not care; I felt I could handle it. While I was in there, the sisters came knocking. He did not answer, and they eventually went away. I pretended to be asleep. He took down my pants and performed oral sex on me. I was ten years old. It scared me a lot because the feelings were so intense. He tried to put his penis in my mouth, but I would not open my mouth. I pretended to wake up and said, "Oh my God! What are you doing?" I jumped up and pulled up my pants. He sat on the side of the bed like a little kid while I reprimanded him. I told him not to let those girls in again and that he had to give me more money, $5.00 to be exact, every time I was to come and knock.

I remember thinking to myself, *$5.00 is a lot of money*. This behavior gave me a lift although it was very stupid and dangerous. I could have lost my life, and no one would have ever known what happened to me. After a few days, my friends started saying that he wasn't answering them. I was glad; I had accomplished my goal. Within two weeks, he closed down his store and moved. That was the last of him. I did not realize that I had been molested until I got to therapy later in life. That was the worst year ever. Or so I thought. Another thing happened that summer. One of my mother's closest friends, a family man, sexually approached me. All of these things happened, but I didn't tell anyone. I just kept it to myself and stayed away from the pervert. I dealt with these issues after a lot more heartaches and devastating experiences that later made me feel that I was about to have a nervous breakdown. Then I got help. Now, when I look back on it all, I know it's only because of the Grace and Mercy of God that I am not in a crazy house or jail, having killed someone by now or dead myself. These experiences damaged me, but they pushed me closer to God. I always called on the Lord and asked him to forgive them. I had become a selfless person, and that's why I believe God has shined his face upon me.

CHAPTER 4

Fall and Burn

<u>My sister, Debra; my brother, Dee; a friend; and I, at thirteen</u>

It seemed that after that year, I blacked out for three years. The next thing I remember is that we moved again, and then I was thirteen years old. I forgot to mention earlier that through all of these experiences, I had asthma attacks quite frequently. I remember going back and forth to the emergency room and receiving shots to be able to breathe. The doctors told my parents that I would grow out of it. I did. In this particular neighborhood, they had a lot of kids. As I previously stated, I needed a lot of stimulation to not get bored. It seems that when I got bored, I became self-destructive. Well, since I have the type of personality that can relate to young and old, I never had a problem making friends or getting boyfriends. People seemed to naturally like me even when I didn't want to be bothered. Because I had been so damaged at a young age, I would oftentimes retreat within myself. I felt safe and secure there. In this neighborhood, I saw many possibilities to grow, cheat, hide, learn, and also crash and burn. I felt like I was in a candy factory and a haunted house at the same time. My appetite was wide open. I became very risky. Not in a sexual sense but in other ways that would dull my senses and cause me great harm, which much later, I would have to overcome. After I had combed the neighborhood and found where I could start my explorations, I started out by making friends with kids my age. Previously I'd stated that I had no problem asking questions. I knew who were the addicts, the alcoholics, the drug dealers, the pimps, the prostitutes, working people, the slow kids, the smart kids, the promiscuous kids, the abusers, and the perverts. The list went on… Any and every personality type lived there. I was on my way to the most scarring and quickest downfall to occur within the next six years of my life. After I knew who did what, I began my exhibition. Growing up in a poverty-stricken family, I believe my choices became very disheartening. I need to say that one of life's survival tasks for me was being able to care for myself financially. Therefore, my first priority was to get some money. I knew I could not depend on my father, because he drugged or gambled his money away, and as for my mom she did whatever she was told. At age thirteen, I felt I needed to take matters into my own hands. I taught myself how to cornbraid. I then proceeded to ask the little girls if they wanted me to braid their hair. I got several clients, so I became self-sufficient at a very young age. I felt good about myself; I felt proud. I finally had my own money to do whatever I wanted. A year passed, and things were good. I had friends and a lot of people places and things to get into.

Then I was fourteen. And at that tender age, I began to smoke cigarettes, a habit that would last for the next thirty years. Funny thing though, I learned to smoke at ages nine and ten. My sister, Deb, and my cousin, Ann, taught me to smoke with ease. They used to say, "Take a puff, take a swallow of water then, blow it out. No coughing or choking. Nice and smooth. Just like that!!!" I remembered that. Anyway, I got tired of hanging with kids my age and needed more stimuli. I just so happened to meet a grown man named Peter around the corner from my house. We would talk from his window until one day he allowed me in. At that point, I was also drinking beer. So he would give me one. I believe I was an instant alcoholic from the time I picked up my first drink. So at this point in life, I went from hanging with the kids my age, to braiding their hair, and then to Peter's house to drink. School started to bore me. Although I'd told myself I would finish and go to college, I did, but not on time. At this point, my life was like a rollercoaster ride. With all of that going on, I felt I still had to find something else to get into. So I befriended a family whose mom worked at night so their house became a "hang out" house. You can imagine what happened! I got involved with one of my friend's brothers. One day, he raped me, and I never was the same. He was fourteen and I fifteen. I became pregnant. He was not nice to me afterwards. He only treated me nicely when he wanted something. There I went, gullible and people pleasing again. I lost that baby to a miscarriage at seven months. My mom took me to St. John's Hospital in Brooklyn on Atlantic Avenue and just left me there. I was in labor with excruciating pain. I felt so alone. I had the baby at 8:27 p.m. on January 2, 1975; she weighted only two pounds. Upon finishing the book, I went to the Bureau of Vital Records and found out that my baby had lived for four hours and eighteen minutes until God took her back. The morning after I'd given birth, the doctor came and told me she was gone. I was so unhappy. How could God take her after I had prayed and cried all night long? Nevertheless, she was gone. I had loved her with all my heart. I had named her Nicole. She would have been forty-three years old today. Here's a copy of her birth certificate.

Needless to say afterwards, I felt so dirty and took shower after shower to "feel" clean. I wanted to have a funeral, but my mother said, "Oh, Leslie, please! You're just a kid!" How does a parent just shrug off something that important like that? I needed therapy in the worst way, which I ended getting much later to close this chapter of grieving. That's one of the reasons why, to this day, I have a problem with experiencing true intimacy. I find it irritating. I was told that it is because of my first sexual experience and how demeaning it was. It's funny though, I have three children and after they were conceived—except for my daughter—I didn't feel a need to be with the fathers. It's like, *OK, I conceived; now you can go.* What's that about? Maybe my womb experiences replaying itself? I wonder… After the miscarriage, I blamed myself and began to drink heavily. I got high every day to ease the pain of this "not so nice world." Also one of my greatest losses was my baby girl, Nicole. I drank beer, smoked weed, and anything I could get my hands on. I barely went to school; I did leave the house every day for school, but I just never got there.

The dreams I had for myself were shattered. My concept of life was distorted. I became this person who just wanted to survive to get high and erase the pain of all the hurt I was continuing to endure. Anyway, after some time, I outgrew this young boy, who had been the father of my baby. Actually, he shunned me during the pregnancy and after the miscarriage. He got involved with a friend's cousin who used to come over on the weekends. I liked her, and we became friends. So there I went again, trying to get them together while suppressing my own hurt feelings.

Well, another year passed and I saw this pimp, who caught my eye. He was gorgeous with a red and white caddy, fine as wine. Here's a picture of his car.

By this time, I was sixteen. My best friend then was the sister of the guy with whom I'd conceived Nicole. She was a year younger than me, but rather voluptuous. I was still small, short but cute. Anyway, the pimp had a record store and so my good friend and I started going there asking for records, just to get his attention. He was married and had a baby. We called ourselves manipulating him, so we offered to babysit. We were underage, but we would go to help out in the store just to be close to him. He would give us a few dollars and some weed at times. We finally confessed that we wanted to be his whores. Go figure, my dreams were to be a whore or a nun. (I lived my life from one extreme to the other.) But, somewhere, deep down inside of me, I believed in a power greater than myself. I know now that it was God's spirit embedded in me, the entire time. Thank you, God!!! Well, getting back to the year of the pimp. My good friend and I told him of our dream. He laughed and was flattered at the same time. He told me. "You look too young to go on the street." You can work in here (the store.) We worked in the store. One day, a Puerto Rican man who came into the store "propositioned" me, and I consented. We got together this one time, and the next thing I knew he was coming too often. I complained, and the pimp confronted him. An argument broke out, and I did not see him again. Funny thing though, the pimp never tried to turn us out until one night we were babysitting. The pimp was married and had his wife engaging in prostitution. She was a track star who had fallen in love with a fool, who had a sick kind of love for her. She was young as well. I believe she was only eighteen. She already had a trick baby. A trick baby is a black mother and white father. The boy had blue eyes. He was gorgeous. Anyway, we babysat him when he took her to the whore stroll on 42nd Street. Sometimes, I would ride with him when I wasn't babysitting. I would think, *Shit, I still want to be his whore*. One night, he went to take his wife to the stroll; when he came back, he tried to have sex with me. I started to let him but he was so well endowed that I got scared and asked him to stop. So he did. I told him I wanted to go home; it was about two o'clock in the morning.

On the way home, we talked about my family. He realized he knew my father and immediately became distant. I knew something was wrong. Later in the week, I told my friend about what he had tried to do with me. Tears came to her eyes; that's when I knew he must have had sex with her. She looked so hurt, so I lied and told her that I had made it up. She seemed relieved. Later that week, I went to the shop and when I entered, I noticed my friend was dressed like a hooker. I was so mad. She was only fifteen! I ran and brought her sister, Tonya. Tonya had been engaging in prostitution herself to feed her two children, whom she'd when she was fourteen and fifteen, respectively. At that time, she was eighteen. When we returned to the store, Tonya went in swinging, and I left, running all the way home, which was two blocks away. I told myself that it was time to find new friends to hang out with, and I did. When I pondered over all that had happened, I got mad. My friend had become so engrossed with him! I lost my friend to the streets. We never were good friends again. During this time, a new family moved in the neighborhood with older guys, and the guys were cute! All of the girls wanted them. I liked one guy named Mark, who came from Kansas City, but because I was short and petite, he looked at me like I was a little girl. At this time, I was sixteen going on seventeen. He liked my friend Amy, but she did not like him. You know, I used to think, *If I can't have them, I'll still be around them by helping them get who they want.* Wow, there I went people pleasing again! I did a lot of compensating in my life. I'd try to stop it, but I found myself very lonely. Most people are users. Either you use them or they use you. Anyway, Amy did not want Mark. He was upset, so he came to talk to me about the situation. One thing led to another and another. Before I knew it, we were having sex. I really cared for him, and I thought he did for me. Well, Mark had to go home to Kansas City for a little while and while he was gone, I continued to visit his house. I was a friend to the girlfriend of the other brother. He was a weirdo. Because he was tall, he would take advantage of people. I knew that, but I never felt threatened, until one particular day. I was at their house with the brother's girlfriend when he pulled me into another room. I kept fighting to not go. His sister and her boyfriend went into the room as well. His girlfriend tried to help me, but they overpowered her. He ended up raping me. At seventeen, I was raped again! The one thing I remember most was him telling me, while he was inside of me and choking me, "If my dog was a boy, I would let him have sex with you too." I was so scared. I told myself that this would never happen to me again, and I would not return here again. When they finally let me out, his girlfriend asked me what happened and again I lied to spare her feelings from getting hurt. What a weak person I was back then!!! I kept it to myself for two weeks. I told my first baby's father's sister, Tonya, and she made me call the police. I did. They arrested him, and he stayed in jail for a week or two. We went to court and because they lied on me, he got off. They made me look like I wanted it.

Later, when I found the nerve to tell my parents, my father went down the block to talk to the guy who had raped me. When he came home, we had an argument, I couldn't believe my ears: my own father believed them over me! This hurt me so, so bad. Although he was an addict, I believed that they gave him some drugs to keep him quiet. My whole world fell apart. At that moment, I knew I was alone in this world. My own father, who was supposed to protect me and make me feel secure, had committed the ultimate betrayal. I hated him with a passion and no longer respected him. One day, we got into it and he called me a slut, his own daughter! I threw a ceramic barrel at his head and missed. I ran into the hallway, where he caught me, pinned me up against the wall, and began choking me. My mother got him off of me. That's when I thought I was going to lose my mind. I then began to run away from home. My mind was racing a mile a minute. I used to think I must be adopted to be in a household like this. God must have made a mistake. I did not belong with these people. I believe that because of all of this, I have been so overprotective of my own children. I refused to let this happen to my kids. I know they think I'm overprotective of them, but once they read this book, they'll understand. My daughter tells me now that she does understand. She sees all of the harm that has come to some of her cousins and friends who are of her age. In spite of all the hurt and injustice I received, I would read my little green Bible, *The Book of Psalms*. From reading that book, the Grace and Mercy of God kept me sane. It kept me from killing those who caused me hurt, pain, and suffering. While writing this book, I wrote an excerpt about what I thought about my father.

"What I think about my father."

Well, let me start by saying I really didn't think much of him. He was a womanizer. Although he was absent a lot due to frequent incarcerations,

I know I didn't care much for him. He had an addictive personally. When I was little, I didn't see him until I was five years old. One day, my mom said: "This is your father and his name is Eddie." He never talked very much. I remember at different ages all the way up until I was grown up, he was in and out of our lives. I felt happy when he was gone; I felt at peace. When he was around, it was a lot of tension. He was a butcher by trade so I admired him for that, but his working was inconsistent. I remember when I was between thirteen and sixteen, he was around selling, using, and gambling away the little finances we had. At thirteen, I saw his works in his coat pocket. I was shocked and vowed never to use drugs. Nevertheless, that was my plight, soon as I began using. He stole toys from us to get a fix or to pay people off. I remember one time these men came to our house to beat him up. It was so scary. I felt betrayed and deprived. I vowed not to get a man like that. I tried not to. I never respected him. I hardly said anything to him for years. He was too high strung. I felt fear and rage toward him. However, I never stopped completely trying to have a relationship with him. When I was in my late twenties, my father came and stayed with us for a while. He never accepted the fact he was an addict. He was a wrathful person. I had my two children at this time and I would buy a ninety-six-count box of Pampers for my newborn. One day when I came home from work, they were gone. He stole my baby's diapers—to buy drugs, I guess. It took a while for me to talk to him again. Then again, in my early thirties, we began to talk on a regular basis. By this time, I was in the grips of my alcoholism, weed, and cocaine addictions. I confided in him, and at that point he gave me words of wisdom. When I was thirty two, he died. I felt we were beginning to get a little closer, but then he was gone. God has blessed me to not hold grudges. I wanted to, but as time passed, the hurt disappeared and empathy set in. I know it's God's way of showing his love for me. Moving forward, the abuse from my environment continued.

Mark came back from Kanas City, and I don't know why I didn't tell him about the rape. There again, not wanting to hurt him, I kept it to myself. Well, his brother painted a different picture. You know, they say little people have this Napoleon complex. I believe we would never have it, if people bigger than us did not try to take advantage of us. One day, Mark confronted me about the rape. He was upset and didn't believe me even though he knew his brother was malicious. We were outside at the time, and he took my shoe off and ran to the building. He told me to come on the stoop. I knew he was going to try something. And he did. He pulled me inside the house and tried to have anal sex with me. The pain was excruciating. My anal area was throbbing, burning, and felt like it was on fire. I was so raw and swollen; eventually he stopped because he couldn't get it in. By this time, his cousin, the brother who had raped me, and a fat friend of theirs, came in. He let them open my legs and look up into my vagina. I was screaming and telling him that I thought he cared for me. He whispered into my ear, "I won't let them hurt you." But they already were. Then he said: 'If you want them to leave you alone, you have to screw my fat friend," and so I did. Afterwards, I got away and went home. Time went on and there was a rumor I had claps, which is an STD (sexually transmitted disease). I didn't feel anything because someone had to have given it to me. I asked my sister to take me to the health station in downtown Brooklyn, and I got treated. After all of this, Mark eventually moved down the block on the main street. When I would pass by, he would tell me to come up-stairs. I said, "No, not after what you did to me." Two months later, at age seventeen, I found out I was pregnant for the second time. It felt like years had passed in just a matter of months. When I informed my mom that I was pregnant again, she said, "You could have the baby." She added, "I know how hurt you were when you lost Nicole." That was what I had named my first born. I told her "No Ma, because I'm not sure who the father is." So, I had an abortion. To this day, I don't regret it. I came to realize that I was very naïve, looking for love in all the wrong places. This was a very destructive time in my life. My life and the world around me seemed so horrid. I could not figure out, for the life of me, why I had to go through this? But I did. By now, my concept of love was all distorted and so I began to write about it....

"What Is LOVE?"
What love means to me. In the Bible, the Lord says in *1 Corinthians* 13:4–7: Love is patient, love is kind. It does not envy, it does not boast, it is not proud.[5] It does not dishonor others, it is not self-seeking, it is not easily angered, and it keeps no record of wrongs.[6] Love does not delight in evil but rejoices with the truth.[7] It always protects, always trusts, always hopes, and always perseveres.

Coming from a hostile environment, I always thought love was an emotional rollercoaster ride. From the time I could comprehend, love was painful. Because of that observation that was embedded in me, I could not receive or give love without it being attached to a harsh or angry response. The one thing, I am absolutely sure, love isn't physical abuse. I saw that as a very young child and somewhere deep inside I knew it was wrong, mean, and selfish. My total concept of love is distorted. After fifty-one years of living, with all the hurt I had endured, my heart was screaming out: I NEED LOVE!!!!!!!! A lot of people say love is not a feeling. I believe love is a feeling, emotions, and actions all rolled up into one. It is the same feeling as to why some women have children. To have someone from within you, to love you, like you, and need to be loved by you. This might be the initial rationale, but after the mind is made up about having the child and the child arrives, this whole rationale goes out of the window. You become attached to the child, and no matter what the circumstances are—good, bad, or indifferent—you love that which is of you. Unconditional love, they call it. Now, is this the same love you should have for your lover, potential mate, or your husband? Some say "It is." I beg to differ. Love manifests at different levels. The love you have for a lover is different from the love you have for your husband. The love I believe you have for a lover is shown to him, because he may be your potential husband. So, therefore, it is attached to a motive. It is real or does it pretend just to get what it wants? Love for your husband, I believe, is admiration. Admiration, that he made you his wife, that he expresses his love and wanting to be there for you, no matter what. Provide, share, and compromise all of his life with you—what a wonderful feeling that must be! This I believe is love. I need to say love creates intimacy. Intimacy meaning, "Into me you see." Seeing and knowing what I need at times even before I know.

Being connected to someone who gets you is very important, and it sustains the relationship.

Communication also plays a big role when it comes to love. If you have difficulty expressing yourself, it will hinder the relationship. Compromise is another important value one must have to keep the relationship going. The lack of compromise results in going from relationship to relationship. Love cannot survive without compromise. Sometimes, you have to give tough love. Tough love to your children will in turn have a positive outcome in the long run. Although your children may feel bad during your display of this necessary behavior, they really don't know it hurts you just as bad as it hurts them. I found out that people have a hard time doing this. However, sometimes it's necessary to save a life, inspire a life, or enlighten one. It takes strong faith to believe that this works. I had to do this, and I am still doing it. I look at my thirty-three-year-old son, and it took him a long time to grasp life and make the positive choices that shifted him into manhood. It took a while for him to get it together, but he is working through it. You know self-love is the most profound love there is. How are you to love everyone as yourself? People have difficulty loving themselves. Life can get so complicated at times, and we have a tendency to get caught up in other people's lives that makes us lose focus on ourselves. When that happens, we become bitter, angry, and inflict pain on ourselves all over again. So now, here we go again, learning to love ourselves. You cry out to stop the hurt, and you're off and running to the races with your feelings again. Who will love you back to yourself? Only the Grace and Mercy of God can bring such a love for self. So now, here you are again, trying to recollect yourself. Find yourself again? When does it end? When does the new kick in? When does the cycle end never to return? Does it suppress itself until the next time?

After the previous drama, I began to drink even more. I had to endure the guy who raped me, who called me names for two whole years. Finally, at the age of nineteen, we moved to Bed-Stuy, "do or die," they called it. I had some cousins down the block from where we moved. I would go to visit them from time to time. I would often visit my old neighborhood, and visit some of my friends there as well. While in my old neighborhoods, my friend Amy's brother, Mitch, always tried to talk to me. He was six-feet tall. He had been trying to talk to me since I was thirteen, when I had first moved in the neighborhood. I did not like him. This seemed to be a pattern in my life. The guys that would pursue me were always the ones whom I did not like. Go figure. Eventually, I would give in to them and in the long run, the reason would show up why I shouldn't have. God gave me the spirit of discernment however; I just didn't use it when it came down to intimate relationships. Duh! Anyway, one night this guy, who later would be the father of my third child, approached me and said, "Hey Les, would you like to get some beer?" I said, "Sure." So he and I went to the store and got a bottle of Old English. That was the beer I liked. We went back to talk and drink. I found out that Mitch was very bright and intelligent. I am always a sucker for intellectuals, knowing now it's all part of the game. Well, one thing led to another and another, and before you knew it...Mitch began to kiss me very gently. I felt like he was being gentle not to frighten me. He knew some of my story, so I felt safe. First, we kissed and he began to loosen my clothing. I let him and didn't say a word. When he entered me, I felt like we belonged together. It was hot, juicy, and electrifying. We had a passionate night, and for the first time I felt like someone made love to me. It was beautiful. When we finished, I felt like I was lying on a white cloud in the sky. I always looked at the clouds and thought they were like fluffy pillows. When I snapped out of it, I put my clothes on and told him I would see him later. Immediately, I looked for my running buddy, his youngest sister. She had been downstairs, drunk sleep. I told her what happened; she seemed upset with me. I could not understand why. Anyway, I did not care. I enjoyed it and was not going to let anyone spoil it. As

I was leaving for home, he walked me to the train. All the way home, I visualized about the evening we had—smiling while taking the long train ride home.

CHAPTER 5

Open Your Eyes, Fool

As time went on, Mitch and I continued to sneak around. We sneaked around, because he had a girlfriend. I kept telling myself, I'm just having fun. Mitch and I spent a lot of time together. We laughed, had mad passionate sex, and shared our stories just the two of us. We enjoyed each other's company. Sometimes, we would go to his father's kitchenette around the corner from my house and stay there all weekend, just him and I. We'd gotten close, or so I thought, until one day he told me his girlfriend wanted to get married. Oh, I left out a little something. She had also had a baby with him. I was crushed. I had been so damaged from past experiences. This was devastating in a different way. I did whatever was presented to me at the time without once thinking of the consequences to others or myself. I told him to go ahead and marry her because if I had had a baby with him, I would have expected him to do the right thing and marry me. I thought to myself, *What a stupid answer!* Mitch said, "Well, I'm not going to do it." I believed Mitch, but when the day of the wedding came, I was discombobulated. My cousin came over to keep me company. I cried and cried, trying to make sense of this unbearable pain I was feeling. Around 2 p.m., there was a knock at the door. Shocked and puzzled, there he was, Mitch in his tuxedo telling my mother that he needed to see me. My mother told him he was crazy and asked him to get away from her door. He wasn't alone; his best man was with him. My ego kicked in; I was angry that he had gone and got married. Mitch and his best man went downstairs and stood in front of our building. My cousin and I sat on the fire escape. Mitch begged me to come downstairs. I cried and cried but refused. I kept saying, "Go back to your wife." I didn't even think about her, how humiliated she must have felt that he left his wedding reception to come all the way across town to see me. I was caught up in my feelings. Mitch and his best man stayed out there until 12 a.m. the next morning. Finally, they left. I would never cry so much again until later in life. At that point in my life, I became emotionally numb. Every time I thought about Mitch getting married, I cried. I had become so emotionally attached to Mitch because in spite of his womanizing, he was good to me. I didn't realize how much I was being emotionally and physically manipulated. Out of desperation, thinking so low of myself, believing this insane relationship was LOVE. My concept of love was so distorted! As weeks went by, I could not shake my feeling of attachment to Mitch. Week three, I called Mitch to come meet me. He did, and we talked and talked. From that moment on, we resumed our relationship like it never ended. At this time, I was twenty. All of this in one year. WOW, so much drama! I was so used to living on the edge that this wasn't any different. Mitch and I stayed together for the next six years, until reality set in. What a rude awakening that was! Because of my early experiences in relationships, my concept was so distorted up until today. The Almighty God had to really work on me! Once we reconnected, Mitch and I became inseparable. He married her on paper, but he was married to me in every sense of the word. We were in our own little world. I wanted Mitch wholeheartedly and thought I loved him so much that I wanted to have his baby.

One day, I looked at myself in the mirror. My spirit began to talk to me right there in that mirror. "What are you doing? You are going to kill yourself. What happened to your aspirations and dreams? You need help or you will die." The spirit of the Living God was speaking. I began throwing up blood. Mitch and I used to drink a lot, and I wanted to stop so badly. Why? I wanted things: Mitch, a baby, and a family life. I went to an alcoholic program to try to get myself together. You should never do anything for other people but only for yourself because if you get help for any other reason than to help yourself first, it won't last. Well, I went to the program for one whole year, and I continued to drink. One day, I got sick and tired of being sick and tired, and confessed everything to my counselor. She said she knew. I requested to go away to a Sober Program out of Brooklyn, NY. I did. By this time, I was twenty-one years old.

Twenty-one years old, making decisions
that would impact my life, forever.

CHAPTER 6

Listen Carefully

Finally, I was beginning to learn who I was, what I wanted, and where I thought I wanted to go. I went to a program in Staten Island. This is where I found out what career I eventually decided to pursue: occupational therapy. What better way to help you with your troubles except to help someone else, right? While in this facility, I had the opportunity to work with an occupational therapist on Friday nights with patients from "Willow Brook," a facility that housed physically deformed and mentally challenged children. We took them in this big pool at the facility in which I stayed. I had a client named "Lucy." She was a teenager who had what you call Bird Syndrome (Seckel Syndrome). Inside the small head is a very small brain, which

causes developmental delay and later mental re-
tardation. Lucy's head was shaped like a beak.
She was about three-feet tall. She could not talk
and was built like a grown woman. She was
sixteen years old at the time. Another woman
and I rolled her on a tire in the pool. So, every Friday we sang "Rock-a-bye Lucy." After
two weeks, when one night, we sang, and she
hummed "rock a bye baby" with us. We were
ecstatic! That's when I decided to pursue occupational therapy. When I was at Staten Island,
Mitch came to visit me there. We were like rab-
bits every time we saw each other. We went
outside on the grounds, and Mitch wanted sex.
We had sex right there in the bushes, and until
this day I believed I conceived Anika. When I
came home, I continued to attend the program
until I finished. I then found out a little later I
was pregnant. I told Mitch, and he told me to
have her. He said: "I want you to have it and
don't pressure me to leave my wife but I am
going to be with you." He kept his promise. My
thought process was so distorted. "How could

I want someone else's husband?" But I did. I got more than I bargained for. As I look back, I guess it's because he made me feel protected and he was a good provider despite him having another family. He taught me a lot. I never wanted to share, but I wound up sharing anyway for seven years of my life, from nineteen till I turned twenty six. I loved Mitch with all my heart. I still find myself thinking about how much fun and the crazy times we shared. I have never loved another like that. I find that when I "feel "too much, I run or sabotage the relationship. Eventually, Mitch and I broke up on bad terms. Our love could not sustain the hurt we inflicted on each other. In spite of everything that happened to me throughout my life, as I look back on it now, I was a prayer warrior. I often prayed and asked, "God please help me!" I believe that because I prayed sincerely to the Lord, He was always there for me, in spite of my choices and decisions. The relationship between Mitch and I took off so sweetly. While pregnant, I stayed with my mother. I used to stay with my sister Debra, but she stayed out a lot and had this guy named Ted who would harass me, making me very uncomfortable. I did not want to tell Mitch, because he would hurt him. So I kept it to myself. Nine months passed, and I had Anika. I felt I needed my own apartment so I went to get public assistance. Since I was eligible, I was able to get an apartment, paid for by the city. I moved out of my mom's house when Anika was three months old. I was twenty-two at the time, and I've had my own place since then. I felt so liberated being in my own apartment. Mitch moved in as well. We were in love, but he had a dark side. He would have tantrums and act crazy for no reason. I would just look at him. I would never show him that I was afraid. Although I was a little, I believed he did it to make me fear him. Around this time, my mom would come and visit. One day, she came by and asked me for some funds. I was grateful I could help my mom. I noticed she was holding her chest and coughing a lot. So I asked her, "Mom, what's going on? You look like you're in pain." She replied, "I've been going to the doctor and taking some tests. I'm waiting for the results." I said, "Ok, well, let me know what he says." She replied "no problem," and then left.

As time passed, I visited my mom and she did not look like herself. She would not tell me what was wrong. It's so important to tell family what is going on. I noticed her pain and suffering in December. In the following March on her fiftieth birthday, she was out of it and had to be admitted to the hospital. I remember the day she died. Five months after I left her home, my mom was gone. I was twenty-two years old with no more moms. I've been all alone without a mother figure since then. My mom suffered and wasted away to bones. Her body seemed like it was disintegrated. No one would tell us what was wrong with her. Her sisters and brothers came from all over—the Bronx, Long Island, Virginia, North Carolina, and South Carolina, but no one revealed to her children the severity of this terminal illness. (cancer in her esophagus).

On her last day in the hospital, my mom tried to talk to me. She must have used all her strength to sit up and try and talk. She said, "He umm, he umm…" I asked, "He who mommy, he who?" She said, "Don't give him any money." I got scared because my mom had not spoken in months. I went and brought the nurse back, who informed me, "When they are like that, they are incoherent." Who *they*? The lady in the bed is my "MOM!" As time passed, my mom just lay there, without saying another word. I couldn't take it any-more, so I went home. My cousin stayed with Anika. When I got back home, Mitch, Anika, and my cousin were there. I was upset. One thing about Mitch was that he was a jokester. So after I told them about my mom, Mitch tried to cheer me up by making us laugh un-til I almost urinated on myself. He could be very, very amusing at times. At that moment, there was a knock on the door. It was my two uncles, my mother's younger brothers. They asked me if could they talk to me. I told them how mommy was trying to talk to me. Very quietly and softly, one of them said, "She's gone." At first, I did not hear them. Then all of sudden, I heard what they said. I got very upset and said, "She was talking to me!" I went into the bathroom to cry. I was not one who would let people see me cry. I must say, on that day, I had a bad, bad feeling in my gut. I mean it was *bad*. I only had that feeling thrice in my life. The day my uncle got shot, the day my mom died, and another time which I'll tell you later in this book. My uncles stayed with me for a while, and we talked about taking my mom down South to be buried in our family plot. And so we did. That was in May 1981. When I returned from South Carolina, I was in for a rude awakening. Mitch had been unfaithful and guess with whom, his wife. She told me she had been in my apartment. I was appalled and felt betrayed, but still wanted Mitch with all my heart and soul. The next four years of my life were a hard lesson and a great blessing.

My mom, Luvenia Green

CHAPTER 7

Take These Chains off of Me

As I previously stated, Mitch had been unfaithful but I had forgiven him. But this time around, Mitch's addiction took off even more. I don't know why, but in a sense I felt obligated to Mitch. He was the only one who had treated me like somebody, or so I thought. From then until now—as I look back on it all—for thirty years it's been very difficult for me to open up in a relationship. Don't get me wrong, I've had many affairs, but not one has added up to a healthy relationship. We will examine why in a moment. During this time, I needed to move. Within the next two years we moved so many times, I lost count. I felt so unstable and trapped. Mitch became very possessive and unpredictable. He would dictate to me what to wear, what not to wear, no lipstick, no shorts skirts, etc. He was clocking my every move. I couldn't go anywhere without him knowing where I was or what I was doing. Everywhere I went, Mitch would find me. Yet, in all of that, he was a womanizer. It took me a long time to come to terms with it and believe that because of the way he treated me, I never suspected that there would be someone else besides me. I gave Mitch my heart and soul. He became very clingy, but he still continued to be a great provider. We were not getting along at all. At times, I hated for him to come home.

A side note: I need to say right here that Mitch was very, very intelligent. You know they say when you're so smart, you're stupid. It's true. I used to say to Mitch: "Mitch, you could be anything you want, but you choose to be an alcoholic. Why?" He never picked up on what I kept saying. Nevertheless, I loved him, until I started going to college. Some of my first classes were psychology courses. Education sure sheds light on things. I began to analyze my own lifestyle. That's when it hit me. I was in a no-win situation. I discovered that I was living a lie with a man that belonged to somebody else. A light went off in my head. What was I doing? I said to myself, *Oh my God, what are you doing?* I started to feel like I was really smothered and shackled. I had to get out. Needless to say, it got really ugly. By this time, my daughter was four and a half. Mitch was getting on my last nerve. Due to his drinking, he lost his good city job. Anyway, days got really, really ugly now. The straw that broke the camel's back was the fact that he had sex with someone in the same building that my cousin lived in. How humiliating it was! I began to lose all respect for him and could not deny the truth any longer. That was it! You know what's funny? I asked him about this particular woman two weeks before he slept with her. He lied to me, just like he's always lied to me, over and over and over again.

Mitch couldn't believe that I was finished with him. He had been after me since I was thirteen. I began the relationship with him when I was nineteen and stayed with him until I was twenty-six. It was time to go. I didn't realize how attached I was until I started making attempts to let him go. I went through some bad withdrawal periods. After some time had passed, Mitch just lost it. He harassed and stalked me. This is when I "really" realized how obsessed he was with me. It became very, very scary. In the middle of all of this, which made matters worse, I met someone. We got together. I never had had a one-night stand before this time. Well, guess what? I got pregnant with my middle son. Now, some people might ask "Why did you keep the baby?" I had my son because I wanted him, and I knew it was my boy. The sad, complicated part about all of this was that it could have been Mitch's son or my one-night stand's son. So, the next seven months and three weeks were torture. No DNA was done. I was so afraid he would hurt me because prior to my delivery, Mitch had been harassing me, threatening me, chasing me up and down the street. He had even pushed me down while I was pregnant, pushed his way into my house, snatched our daughter, got on a bus, and the cops had to take them off the bus to return my daughter to me. All of this I endured, yet never once did I wish anything bad on him. Mitch kept telling me how he loved, and how he *really* loved me. But at that point in my life, I loved Leslie a little more. Well, let me go back and tell you what happened when he came to the hospital after I had delivered my second baby. It was the last ten minutes of visiting hours. I got a knock on the bathroom door, and my hospital roommate announced, "You have a visitor." I was very pissed. I don't understand, to this day, how he got up there so late. Anyway, I was actually afraid for my life. I knew he had come to see if the baby I had had was his. We went into the hallway, and of course I acted like I wasn't afraid but I was very terrified. For half an hour, he asked me over and over whether the baby was his. Finally, because I was tired and in pain, I confessed that the baby was not his. He said, "Can I see him?" Because he had four daughters, my daughter being the youngest, he was yearning for a son. Anyway, he saw the baby and smiled. He asked me if I wanted him to take me home. I did not want any problems, and I was again in so much pain from my breasts swelling up with milk, I said yes.

The next day Mitch came and took me home. Since my baby was premature, he had to stay in the hospital for a couple of weeks. I was grateful, even though I wanted my baby home; this gave me an opportunity to relax and get myself together. Now, my son's father, whom I found out the night I delivered the baby, was only twenty one. What a shock!!! The one-night stand was very immature on both our parts. He had lied about his age until the day I had our son. I was devastated with myself. I had to make some hard choices. Some I'm not too proud of, and some I'm glad I did. Anyway, when I got home, he called. I remember Mitch peeked through my bedroom door, while I was on the phone with him. He asked if I wanted him to come by, but of course I couldn't have him come over while

Mitch was there. I was just finding out that my son's father wasn't honest with me at all. Although I had many distorted relationships I always had hope that one day God would bless me with the man he wanted me to have. Weeks passed, and my baby came home. (I need to say here that I had a cousin staying with me at the time. In a way it was helpful; in a way it wasn't.) I became ill, shortly after my son came home. I went to the hospital, and I had a very bad infection. My God, when the doctor examined me, I thought I was going to die. I was in so much pain, it was unbelievable.

The doctor said I had the infection during my pregnancy and that was why it was so painful. Finally, I got treated and felt much better. I was enjoying my baby boy and my life. Then, things began to take a turn for the worse. Mitch began to harass me again, stalk me, and physically abuse me even more. Again, I was afraid for my life, but I continued to go to school. I was determined that I was going to get my degree; that way, I would be fully self-supporting. I realized from attending college and taking psychology classes that I had been restrained mentally, physically, and emotionally. I felt like I was in chains. Now, it was time to take them off. All hell began to break loose. Mitch was enraged that I didn't want him anymore. He was furious with me. I had had enough with Mitch. There was no turning back. I reached out to my family for guidance and strength. My family has a spiritual gift of discernment and vision to foresee. God has blessed us that way. I asked my cousin if she felt Mitch was going to hurt me. She said, "Yes, but he is not going to kill you." I was even more afraid for my life. One day I was going to school—and I don't know about anyone else, but my gut flips when something is about to happen or has happened. That day, I got a very, very bad feeling in my gut. I only had this feeling twice in my life. The day my mother died and the day Mitch hurt me. Mitch's sister was watching my children. I called from school to ask if Mitch was around. She said that he was asleep. I told her to get the kids ready, so I can take them home when I come.

Once I got there and sat down, Mitch woke up and walked by me with hatred in his eyes. I tried to be brave. I didn't want to rush out, because I knew he would follow me. So, I proceeded to change my three-month-old son. As I have stated earlier, Mitch has four daughters, and our daughter is his youngest. He wanted a son so bad. He stood over me as I changed the baby. I knew he wouldn't hurt him. He loved children. I was being careful with the baby, because he had gotten circumcised just days before. They didn't do it when he was born because he was so little, having been born at seven months and three weeks. After that, I walked out into the hall, and he followed me there. I stood by the banister in the hall. The tenants from the third floor were out in the hallway. They told Mitch to leave me alone and that I didn't want him anymore. This agitated him even more. They finally left the hallway. I heard this small voice say to me: YOU NEED TO MOVE, BECAUSE IF HE HITS YOU, YOU ARE GOING TO DIE. I quickly moved from in front of the banister, to placing myself in front of the bedroom door. The next thing I knew, Mitch was saying: HERE IT IS, I WANT TO FUCK YOU AND YOU WANT TO FUCK SOMEONE ELSE. He punched me through the door. The door opened, and I flew like a football into the middle of the floor. It felt like he broke my face. Mitch was still standing at the door. He shook his head and said, "OH MY GOD, What did I do? OH My GOD!!!! LET ME SEE… I THINK I BROKE YOUR NOSE. How could I do this to you?" I was crawling to get away from him. His sister, my daughter, and my cousin came into the room, and they all screamed at the same time. I was furious and scared that he was going to finish me off. I wanted to kill him. I told my cousin to help me kill him. I told her I was going to stab him, but if I didn't get him good he was going to kill me. I remember her saying, "I'm scared." I was mad at her, but now in hindsight, I am grateful. I would have been in jail had I done what I said. I asked her to go to the hospital with me. She agreed to go with me. Mitch's sister said she'd call the police.

They took so long to get there. This was in 1985. I began to panic and told them I was going to the hospital, which was three blocks away. I told my cousin to come, and Mitch said, "NO… I'm going." I felt like he was going to finish me off on the way. As we proceeded to the hospital, he asked to see my face. He looked at me and said, "Boy I'll never get some now." That was so profoundly alarming to me! He was concerned about sex, and I was concerned about my injury. When we got to the hospital, they took me right in. I informed the nurse that he had done this, and they called the cops.

The cops came and were very short with him. I thought Mitch would overpower them. He was crazy like that. The officers came to the back, and they asked me whether Mitch was the man who did this to me. My spirit told me not to look at him. Mitch asked me, "What's going on, Leslie?" The cops asked, "Is it him?" I shook my head yes. They took him in. He was arrested. I had many orders of protection and yet, it still didn't protect me. Some might say I deserved it, but no one deserves to be physically injured by the one they thought they loved. NO ONE. I do believe I was wrong and should have left Mitch alone when he got married, but growing up without boundaries, anything goes. I need to say right here. After this horrific experience, I vowed not to get involved with married men and I didn't ever again. If I found out, I left them alone. I felt sorry for Mitch. He was possessed by demons that would not let him rest until they killed him. In the Bible, it's there plain as day. Scripture: "The enemy comes to kill, steal and destroy." His ultimate goal is to kill you, but he will settle for making you miserable if he can't. So, as I looked in the mirror, I cried each time I looked at my face. I had to bathe my face with warm water and salt or ice for three whole months to decrease the swelling. My eye was bloodshot red. I tried to get the actually picture from police department, but it was already destroyed. The pain was unsurpassable. This is what I looked like…

TURN THE PAGE!!!

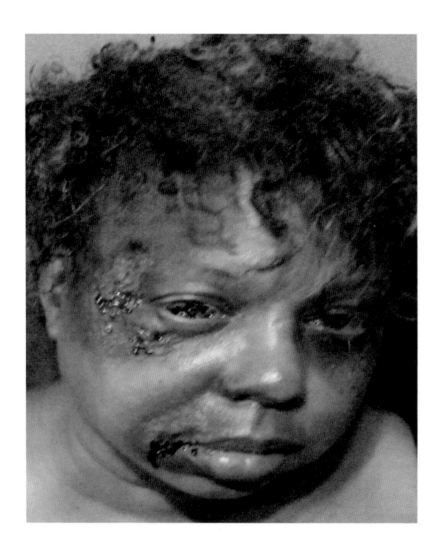

This is not the original picture. A make-up artist did this re-enactment named:
"Iesha Nicole Johnson"
Web address: *GetGlambyGlamazon.com*

I was traumatized. I couldn't believe this! The man I loved and for whom I blithely disregarded everyone. How could he hurt me like this? Me? The one that he loved so much. The one I trusted with all my heart. After this very horrifying experience, I became an introvert. We went to court for two years. During this time, the district attorney informed me that I should let Mitch go because he said he would be in jail plotting how to kill me. I couldn't believe my ears. How do you let someone go, someone who has hurt you this bad? I refused to give in. After the two years, they gave him a conditional discharge to enter an alcoholic program. Guess what, and it did not include staying away from me. Go figure. I knew he would stay away from me because he knew I would have tried to kill him if he didn't stay away. He still wanted to see our daughter. So he took me to family court. They granted him visitation rights, but he had to visit her through my brother or his sister. By the time Mitch was thirty-four, he was dead. He drank himself to death. God rest his soul. He never got the message of recovery... Maybe, if he went to jail, it might have saved his life. I saw Mitch three months before he died. He told me he still loved me, and I didn't say a word. My spirit said to me: "Do not say anything." Although Mitch was caught in the grips of alcoholism, I do believe he loved me with all he had. I prayed that God gave him the rest he deserved...

CHAPTER 8

Unravel My Soul

Unfortunately, I got away broken, battered, and dam near insane. However, I was still alive. So, at this point in life, I had two kids and my son's father wasn't any better. He was young and foolish. So again, I began to beat myself up, yet I continued to go to school and graduated. I stayed home with my son for one year, before I started working. I needed the work to maintain my sanity. I got my first job in occupational therapy at a local hospital. Finally, I could put into practice what I had learned. I loved helping people. As time went on, I continued to smoke weed but not drink, because I knew I couldn't handle it. So, I would put the kids to bed and then smoke and watch TV until I fell asleep. From time to time, my son's father would come by. I can't believe

I had such low self-esteem to allow this kid to come and use me. Some might think I had this baby to be with this guy. But that wasn't the case. I had my son because I wanted a boy and a girl. God blessed me with that desire of my heart. I was working and loving it. My first job was all I ever wanted. Therapy in the eighties was *therapy*. We were able to give the clients what they needed: one-on-one treatment, spending quality time with them, implementing ADL activities such as dressing, grooming, toileting, upper extremity activities and relearning how to practice good hygiene skills, etc. Also, the rehab department worked as a team: occupational, physical, recreational and speech therapies. Oftentimes, we would put on shows as part of a team effort. We had a lot of fun. The clients appreciated that we worked together and trained them to go back out into the world to function as normally as possible. I enjoyed my life, but something was missing. I couldn't put my finger on it. What was it? My mind, at the time, was to have it all: the job, the kids, and a husband. That's it. A significant other! Although, I was sexually involved with my son's father, it wasn't the relationship I wanted. He didn't care for me like that. He didn't even come to visit me on a regular basis. I don't know what I was thinking; I just wanted intimacy no matter what the cost. Since I couldn't have what I wanted, I threw myself into my work. I believe I became a little resentful even though I never had a problem meeting guys or dating. It's just not the same when you're not in a relationship. It's just instant gratification similar to what drugs do—for a moment's pleasure. As a result, I continued to have flings and take care of my kids. It became humdrum to me. Every night, I would get my bag of marijuana, smoke, watch TV, and converse with myself. Not knowing that was insanity. I became very depressed and started making worse choices. Even though I was in this state of mind, I continued to pray to a power greater than myself to relieve me from all the hurt, disappointments, and bad choices I made for my family and me. I believe the Lord heard me. Although it took many, many years, the Lord restored me to sanity. Time passed on. I was thirty-two then and my drug addiction had gotten worse. I started to drink again, smoked marijuana, snorting and smoking cocaine. My world was falling apart. I used to get drunk and couldn't go to work while stoned out of my mind, but I did. It was only through the grace and mercy of God that I made it through the day. One day my supervisor saw me and asked, "What is going on with you?" I couldn't hide it anymore; I needed help badly. She informed me that I was in the union, and I should go and seek help. I agreed but in the back of my mind I was thinking, "She must be out of her mind." I went home in a cab because I was so stoned out of my mind, I could barely walk. When I sobered up, I thought about what she said, so I decided to call the union and make an appointment. Let me back up a minute. Before I decided to go to the union, I was walking around in my apartment and my spirit said, "You are going to destroy everything you worked hard to get. You need some help!" I was like, "Oh my

God!" That scared me. I immediately called the union and made an appointment. I went to my appointment and spoke with a counselor. I was appalled at what he said. He told me that I was putting the blame on everybody and everything else but myself. He told me that I was the problem and not anyone else. I remember laughing at what the man was telling me. I said, "There isn't anything wrong with me; everybody is getting on my nerves." How many of us have felt that way? Be honest with yourself, hmmm? As time went on, I wanted this man to prove to me that I was the problem. So I followed the program he required for me to go through. I was mandated to go to the union meetings once a week. I did that for seven months. Now, because I was in denial about my addiction, of course I was not going to AA (Alcoholics Anonymous). From what I remember, people in AA were very old and I'm young. I didn't need that, so I decided to go to NA (Narcotics Anonymous). When I went to my first meeting, I looked around the room. I noticed that there were slogans up on the walls, and a "KNIHT" sign was upside down. I wanted to fix it but I was afraid to move. So I just sat there. It was a good meeting. People were telling some juicy stories, and because I'm nosey, they sounded good. I was excited but not eager to go back. They had a lot of guys in there that "looked" clean, sober, and smelled good… That was a turn-on for me. It took me a while before I made another meeting. Funny thing though, I started running into people that were in recovery, and that's how I made the decision to start attending meetings on a consistent basis. It took a little while for me to lose the desire for drugs and alcohol, but I guess it was time. As time went on, I started getting turned off from attending meetings. I went to an anniversary, and the leader made me feel so embarrassed. She reprimanded me because I wasn't familiar with the format. I immediately got offended. I vowed to never attend an NA meeting again. About this same time, I had my first car, so I decided to start attending AA meetings instead, since my first drug of choice was alcohol. I began to open up a little bit and managed to establish some friend-ships. I got a sponsor in the beginning, but she was too busy to really help me. So I got a new sponsor, and she was fun to work with. We en-joyed each other's company. I was very serious minded, and she made the surroundings good for me to open up. I enjoyed my new life. I had a lot to learn. How to express myself and love myself for who I am. There were times when I would be happy, sad, confused, and angry—just a ball of emotions. I didn't pick up drugs again from all of it. Thank God for the strength, and I know it was his grace and mercy that brought me through.

CHAPTER 9

Speak to Me, Lord!

Six years passed. I continued to make the meetings. By this time, I felt pretty good about myself. Still, something was missing. By then, I was thirty-seven. Hanging out, partying, and enjoying my time in recovery and my newfound friends. During this time, I was trying to move from my apartment in Bed-Stuy for a while and all of a sudden I got a letter to move from Bed Stuy to Canarsie. The kids were perplexed. They did not want to move. I did, because it was getting really rough around there. Anika was already in high school, almost ready to graduate, and I just didn't want Kashif growing up over on that side of town with all the stuff going on. God answered my prayers. Before I moved, I met a guy. He seemed very nice. We got along fairly well. He had a little attitude problem, but I let it go. We liked the same music. He had a car and didn't mind picking me up. Although I have my own car, it did feel good for somebody to drive me around. He didn't appear to be stingy. This changed very quickly though. Sometimes we deceive ourselves. I thought I had found the one. But when you choose and not God, all hell breaks loose. Little things started happening. Things like phone calls telling me that the guy I had met was not telling me the truth; finding some root powder sprinkled with honey on it outside my apartment door, which was scary. But that didn't stop me from seeing him. I really liked him. He would leave and come right back. One day, I was walking through my living room and I heard: "He's not telling you everything." So I confronted him about it and of course, he tried to divert my attention. He said to me, "Yes I am. Look, I bought you something." It was a nice leather bag. So whatever I had heard, it went out the window just that fast. I continued seeing him. I can't remember what happened, but soon after that I was very upset with him. He tried to talk to me, but I wouldn't let him. As I had mentioned earlier, I was a recovering addict and I was attending meetings regularly. This particular night, I went to a meeting and it was a group anniversary. Group anniversaries are fun. You get to see people you haven't seen in a while, dance, eat, and have fun for free. Anyhow, he came to the group anniversary with someone else. He tried to communicate with me, but I still wouldn't talk to him. I spoke to my sponsor about it; she said, "Well, you should at least talk to him." So I started looking for him. It was very crowded. I saw him going out of the door with the young lady he came with. I was pissed. I called him, and he just didn't turn around. Well, I got very, very, upset. I ran outside, trying to flag him down on the street, and he simply sped off. Now, I was really upset. How could he diss me like that? I jumped in my car and went down a two-way street the wrong way to try and catch him. I was on Glenwood Road and East 32nd Street. I lost my cognizance for a moment. Then

I caught myself. I drove back to the party, but I didn't stay long because I was too dismayed. I kept trying to call him, but he wouldn't answer me. So, I had no choice but to leave well enough alone. I had gotten emotionally involved with him too quickly. All of this was going on in the process of me moving. Therefore, I had to pack and move all by myself with my children. It was packing thirteen years of stuff; oh God, I had a lot of stuff! When we moved into the new apartment in Canarsie, Brooklyn, the kids weren't happy.

Granted that I was depressed about the previous relationship I had just lost, but I was glad I had moved out of Bed-Stuy, Brooklyn. I was still disheartened, and my kids noticed it. My daughter tried to encourage me to go out. I just didn't want to run into him again with someone else. Well, I don't recall how we began to talk again. But we did. So there we were starting to see each other again. Hence, I had the bright idea of having another child, and he agreed. It was very juvenile thinking on my part, to say the least. I don't regret having my child; I just regret picking him for his father.

I just wanted to have a lasting relationship with someone with whom I could grow old with. Needless to say, he was not the one. Immediately after I got pregnant, he started changing drastically. I was a little taken aback at his behavior. I used to tell him that this situation was only temporary. Not only was I dealing with his attitude and behaviors, he was also living with a woman—who had had a child with him as well. He was confused. He just couldn't make his mind up on what he wanted to do. So I made it for him. When my son was born, I stopped seeing him. I became very depressed and couldn't believe I picked the wrong guy—again. Side note: I'm not trying to ignore my part in all of this, because I played a big role. I just thought that at the age of thirty nine, I would have made better choices for myself. When they say, "It gets better with time," it definitely does. During my depression, I was very irritable. I remember when my son was three months old, I got so upset one day. I couldn't believe that I had done this to myself, again. I wrapped up a knife, put it inside the stroller, and went outside to look for his father to kill him. But for the grace of God, I didn't find him. I was devastated. I had had to stop working six months into my pregnancy because the doctors had put me on bed rest. During my pregnancy, my son was laying on a nerve in the back of my right my leg, which would give out on me. Therefore, I couldn't work. I couldn't stand on it without shooting pain down my leg. This is when his father really showed his true colors. To add to my depression, my job insurance wouldn't give me maternal disability until after I had my son. I was distraught. I had two other children and now a baby to support, and his father picked and chose when to give me money for him. I had to go to family court for child support. Of course, he didn't show up, so they based the child support on how much they thought it cost to raise a child in New York City. As time went on, the lady with whom my son's father was living allowed my son to come and

spend weekends with her son. So the two brothers could form a bond. I was grateful for that.
God bless her heart. Even though I got breaks, I
was still down in the dumps. Even though I was
upset when I had to pick him up from there, I
tried not to let it show. I would say to myself,
"You know you don't want his father, so why are
you upset yourself?" I didn't want him because
he cursed a lot, he never took responsibility for
his actions, and his priorities were out of order.
He would argue about stupid things, which I
was not going to spend the rest of my lifetime
dealing with. My son was growing fast. I started
to notice particular behaviors in my son. He
was very active and never wanted to sit down.
He moved around the house like the roadrun-
ner. I brought it to his father's attention. He was
in denial about everything. Since I worked as
a certified occupational therapy assistant, I was
familiar with children who had developmental
delays. I knew something was wrong.

Nevertheless, I had him evaluated and they
said he had attention deficit hyperactivity disorder

(ADHD). This disorder causes one to have a very short attention span, restlessness, inability to sit and eat, unable to retain information, and a gambit of other symptoms. We immediately began to look for special schools that would help him. Let me give you some history. I had placed him in different daycare facilities because I was having some problems handling him. I was so burnt out and overwhelmed, I found a place called Avenue B Christian Day Care. The people were very good with him. When he turned three, I had to look for another schools for him. I got him re-evaluated for a school called the League School, which caters to children with various diagnoses. This school did wonders for him. First, they had him in the classroom with a two to one ratio—two students and one teacher. He could not even sit down to eat a meal. They had to strap him to the chair. Some people say its abuse; I say, it worked. As time went on, they put him in a six-student and two-teacher classroom setting. Then, they moved him to a twelve-student and two-teacher classroom. This school was great

and helped him grow tremendously. He graduated and went on to public school—a classroom
with twelve special education students and
twelve regular education students. When they
decided to do this particular program, I didn't
think it was a good idea at first. It worked for
some kids; but for others, it didn't. My son was
exceptional, thank God. The diagnosis (ADHD)
they gave him was wrong because his cognition
was exceptional. So they put him in a regular
classroom. Early on, I remember when the therapist first came to my apartment, she said that I
needed to take a lot of things off the walls. She
said it overly stimulated my son. So I did. While
my son was doing well academically in school,
his conduct was out of control. He still had tem-
per tantrums. He was overly sensitive and just
being a boy in general. I was so frazzled. While
he was in regular education classes, quite often
the school would call me. This ultimately took a
toll on me. Again, all this while still being challenged myself, with depression and feeling very
overwhelmed.

On a happy note, during this time, my daughter was graduating from high school. I was so proud. She was sixteen years older. My middle son is eleven years older than his little brother. Even though I was happy she was graduating from high school, she was too through with me for having another child. So going through what I was going through with my youngest son's father, my daughter decided that she wanted to stay with my brother. He lives in Bed-Stuy, Brooklyn, and she wanted to be over there with her friends. I was shattered. This was her last year of high school, prom time had come, and I just wanted to get her dressed for the prom. You know, just to have the opportunity to do the "motherly things" that you do when they are preparing for prom, graduating from high school, etc. Well, by the time it was ready for her to go to college that summer, we made up. I was going through a lot that year. It was only through God's grace that I didn't lose my mind.

Getting back to my youngest son and the diagnosis they gave him, even if he was retaining information, he was still had a behavioral problem. As I previously stated, this school called me often. It became extremely exhausting for me. I had to go and find a therapist just for me! I felt like I was about to lose my rationality. My son stayed in that school until the fourth grade. He had reached the point where he didn't even like school anymore. He said people picked on him all the time. I would bring it to the attention of the teachers and the principal every time an incident occurred, but of course they would put it back on him. I was so appalled. One day, my son had a fight right after I had left him at school. I just left the school and received a call telling me to come back. There was a serious incident that my son was involved in. I had to leave work because he had a fight and knocked a boy out. I was shocked. What was going to happen to my son? Straightaway they gave him a superintendent suspension and began the process to put him in another school. Now mind you, I had asked them all that year to change his class, but to no avail. They put him on suspension, which would put him out of school for a few weeks at first. Then he would go to the new school in placed in the save room. He stayed there for a while. I was determined that he would not return to his regular school. I proceeded to write letters to the superintendent of the district and people in the board of education department requesting that he stay at the school that he was transferred to for the duration of the year. I was told "no." After this incident, I got my son a therapist outside of the school system. **"NEVER GET YOUR CHILD A THERAPIST WITHIN THE SCHOOL SYSTEM. THEY CAN USE IT AGAINST YOU."** My son continued seeing the counselor outside school from fifth to eighth grade. She conducted an evaluation on him, and she told me that he was very intelligent. It was so strange because when she told me this, she suggested I inquire about the test for gifted students. I followed up immediately. To my surprise, the test was on the following day. I know it was only because of God that it unfolded like that. So I had him tested. And sure enough he was gifted!

He was accepted into the gifted program at another school and also a charter school. I decided to put him in the gifted program. He did well, but he still was getting into a lot of altercations with his peers. In spite of this, he graduated and went to junior high. While in junior high school, he continued to have drawbacks. With all the changes, going up and down, I found myself leaning closer and closer to despair. I would call on God more and more. I was so fed up with everything and everybody. I just wanted to establish a relationship with my higher power and see where that would lead me. I was at my wit's end. Now, as I was having a conversation with the Lord, I heard, "Take out the play you wrote when your son was a year old and finish it." I was not interested in finishing it. How will that help my hopelessness? As a result, I just put what I'd heard to the side and went on my merry way. I was still trying to do things on my own. I didn't seem to have the drive to do anything else by myself. So, I blocked everybody out. Months later, I spotted a neighbor of mine in the neighborhood park. We began talking about plays. I broke down what I thought I wrote thus far and when she said, "You should take out your play and finish it." That's the day I heard the Holy Spirit speak to me again. I told her I would. I went upstairs, a little excited. One thing about me, if I don't complete something, I don't just throw it away. I found the play in my file cabinet. I began to read it and didn't realize that I had written as much as I did. Then the Holy Spirit started giving me highlights to put into the play. Step by step, I was led to do everything I needed to get the play off the ground. I thought I'd let my daughter type it out nice and neat for me. She came home for a few weeks from school and typed it up. She's a very fast typist. She can type like a hundred words a minute, unlike me—I type with two fingers.

After she typed it, I asked her opinion. She said, "It's good, Mommy, I mean 'really' good." I asked, "Really?" She said, "Yes, Mommy." Again, I was enthusiastic. So I asked the Lord what to do next. I heard "Copyright it." I asked where. I was told to go to the Brooklyn Public Library at Grand Army Plaza. So I decided to take a friend with me. Along the way, I told her this is what I was being given to do from the Lord. So we went to the Brooklyn Public Library at Grand Army Plaza, and I ask for copyright forms. The attendant at the desk said that she didn't have any. There was another person standing behind her, who said, "Yes we do, they're upstairs." I looked at my friend as she looked back at me, and we started smiling at each other. As we headed upstairs, my friend said, "I don't think they're going to let you use that name for your play." I told her, "Oh, yes they will because God gave me that name for my first production, seven years ago." When we reached our destination, I asked again for the copyright forms. The lady behind the desk again stated, "We don't have any more forms." There was a young man behind her who overheard her and quickly intervened, "Yes we do, it's in the purple book on the shelf." I looked at my friend, she looked at me, and we started laughing. So I said, "Look at God!" The young man retrieved the forms I needed and told me to make copies. So I did. My friend and I laughed about it all the way home. It was amazing. God is AMAZING! To know what I heard, step by step, to go to the Brooklyn Public Library Grand Army Plaza to get copyright forms and to almost be deterred. Nevertheless, because God led me there, He was there first. My God, what an awesome experience that was! Even to share the moments with my friend was flabbergasting. As I continued on my journey, I filled out my copyright forms and asked the Lord what to do next. I was late to mail them off. Copyright takes a long time. Around this time, it was like mid-September and I tell y'all, I was on pins and needles waiting for the copyright form to come back to me, stamped and sealed. To know that I have a piece of work in the Library of Congress! Such an honor in the name of the Lord! Although I have written sixteen productions thus far and produced them all, I have six in the Library of Congress. Wow! That's truly amazing. After all that I've been through in my life! But my God is amazing. I can do all things through Christ that strengthens me. I'm still amazed at my progress and the audience that comes to see my productions. I know it's only God's grace and mercy that leads them there. For that, I am truly grateful and honored to present awesome messages from God.

My first production "Father, Where Art Thou?" was copy-written in 2002; however, I didn't have my directorial debut until 2004. I wanted my first production to be pleasing in the eyes of the Lord. A little bit about this play: The concept of "Father, Where Art Thou?" is about two sisters and a brother with their own personal dilemmas. The oldest sister, Theresa, is a God-fearing, married woman who goes to church all the time. Because of her dedication to God, she neglects her husband, Sledge. In turn, of course, her husband looks for attention elsewhere. In the process of him doing this, he contracts HIV. Because of his shame and guilt, he leaves before he is able to give it to his wife. They also have a sixteen-year-old son named John, whom he also neglects due to his shame. John internalizes this and becomes severely depressed. Due to his depression, John's academics fall below average. Theresa informs Sledge and he agrees to see him, but it's too late. John has a fatal accident and dies the same day Sledge keeps his word. How tragic.

Theresa also has a younger sister named Donna, who blames God for all her troubles. She has two sons named Divine and Justice. She leaves them all the time to go out with different men, looking for love in all the wrong places.

However, one thing she does, she makes sure they go to church. Divine doesn't like it and confronts his mom. She puts him in his place before running off on a Sunday to yet another date. When she leaves, he tells his brother his concerns. His brother comforts him as they leave for church.

Theresa and Donna have a brother named George. George has two daughters named Jessica and Janale. Because George didn't marry their mother, Tess, she refuses to allow him to visit his daughters. He confronts Tess all the time about it but she becomes enraged; George continues trying. With the tragedy that happens with John and the help of a young Minister named Saeed, the families find peace in the midst of their personal storms.

This play is ongoing since its debut in 2004. What an awesome God we serve. Although I've put on the play, in all of these years, I've gave all my revenue either to the church, cast members, props, theatre rentals, sound technicians, videographers, etc. I haven't begun to pay myself. I believe maybe on two occasions, I kept very little for myself. My payment is carrying awesome messages from God. To God be the Glory!

CHAPTER 10

Distractions in Pursuit of My Spiritual Journey

Even with all of my current accomplishments, I still felt something was missing. I still yearned for companionship. So one day, I was in the hall smoking a cigarette. I know you're probably saying, "She's doing Gospel plays and smoking?" Yes, I was. Before this experience, I always thought I had to get right first. But that is not the case. You have a relationship with God, so you can get it right. Anyway, the yearning for a relationship just wouldn't go away. While smoking I heard, "So you want to get married?" "Well, when you get mad, you can't ask your husband to leave. That's not how it works." I was shocked; only God knows me inside out.

Wow! After some time I'd gotten so comfortable spending time with Lord, he informed me that I needed to let certain people back into my life. I was reluctant. The peace that I had, I can't even begin to describe! I always had difficulty sleeping, but during those two years, spending time with the Lord, I slept like a baby. As the Lord prepared me for allowing people back in my life, I felt shunned. In hindsight, looking at it, it was the best thing that could have happened to me. The Lord said to me: "You need to learn how to let things roll off your shoulders." He was right. I was so sensitive to everything, and I do mean everything. Even today, at times my doctor says the same thing to me. The only thing now is that I'm able to let things roll off my shoulders much better. Prior to me spending time with the Lord, there was a man whom I began seeing socially. I was told he would be coming back into my life and that I needed to make him work. "Make him work?" I asked. "Yes." I guess what the Lord was trying to get me to do was to make him "earn" me. Well, of course I didn't make him earn me long enough, so the relationship eventually dissolved. This was definitely someone I felt I could have had a lasting, committed relationship with, but I guess I was wrong. I don't know about anyone else, but have you ever had that person whom you really opened up to? Let your guard down? But you become very disappointed because for them it was about the conquest and not true commitment… It's such a devastating disappointment. I told him I was appalled and upset at the outcome because in twenty years I hadn't let anybody in. When people perpetrate a fraud, you end up not making the right decisions for yourself. I'm in my fifties, and this is so ridiculous that men my age and older still haven't grown up to the point that you can't have a serious conversation that leads to a mature, adult relationship. I'm not passing blame. I'm just explaining to you my experience with this situation. I would not want to put anyone down or make someone feel bad deliberately. This is just how I feel about this particular situation. I probably would have never let him come back in my life if he wasn't saying and doing some of the right things. You know, sometimes you're just not meant to be together. But it didn't stop there. I talked myself into seeing him at least twice a year. So, now he's my booty call. Yes, while all of this is taking place, while I'm producing, directing, and writing gospel plays. I had "distractions in pursuit of my spiritual journey." You know, Paul says in the Bible that every time I wish to do good evil is always present. This is so true, and I experienced it. So for the next four years this is what went on. I cried and prayed and asked for forgiveness each time I did it. I felt I had to satisfy my flesh. Yet, all the while I was doing Gospel plays. Jesus said, "He comes to set the captives free." We're all sinners, saved by his Grace and mercy. Unfortunately, these behaviors caused me to beat up on myself. I often cried because I felt so dishonorable. Being the merciful God that he is, he would comfort me in my time of need. I love the Lord, and I won't take it back. Funny thing though, throughout this ordeal, my creative flows was in full swing. The Lord was giving me plays every year. Up until now, I've written twelve productions and three children's books. I have two plays yet to produce and another children's book to publish. As time went on, I knew I had to stop. This behavior was taking a toll on me. Although I had genuine feelings for this brother, the feeling wasn't mutual. I had to get away. You know there is always a ram in the bush. I was often propositioned. So eventually, I accepted it. Subconsciously, I told myself I was having fun. Sounds familiar? So, here I am back again in that secret sexual relationship. The one that I vowed I would never be in again. Now, in this relationship, this guy was one of my confidantes. You know that's the guy you tell all of your secrets to. You know all of his. Well, this secret rendezvous didn't last very long. My confidante began to treat me like all the others. Wow.... was I hurt! Now this time, I really didn't like the feeling so I had to stop myself. I took a trip to Atlanta for Thanksgiving and told my friend about my situation. I told her I was appalled with the way he was treating me. All standoffish and everything. She said, "Well, if he's your friend, why are you offended? You let your feelings get into it." She was right. Why was I upset? I had let my signals get crossed. I didn't want a relationship with this guy because I knew his story and he knew mine. And baby, it's a doozy. That's for him to tell. Anyway, I continued a little while longer with him and I kept receiving the same results. I became part of his harem. I was every three weeks. Now you know! Also, he didn't like to use condoms. I had to insist. When I got sloppy on two occasions, I knew it was time to walk off. No one is going to give up free sex. For me, my spirit always kicks up and convicts me when I'm wrong. I just wish I obeyed before the fact. So I finally let go. I'm not condemning him because I'm just as wrong as he is. However, I am no longer a babe in Christ. I know better. Besides this being a distraction, my youngest son was entering young adulthood. Boy oh boy, what a trip was that! He got involved with a young lady his age. I always try to get involved with my kids' friends to see what's going on in their lives. Anyway, she started going to church with us. I was feeling good about that, but her family background was a mess. She appeared innocent. Well, lo and behold, they had sexual relations. My son went coocoo for cocoa puffs. He became very disrespectful toward me. I couldn't believe his transformation before my eyes. I had to pray so hard not to crack him upside his head. I felt the enemy was trying hard to get me locked up. I'm talking about distractions y'all, trouble on every side. An assignment to get me totally off my course from the destiny God had placed before me. One night, he was supposed to go to the school's banquet. This cost $60 plus his suit, shoes, and carfare. Twelve o'clock came. No son. I called his cell phone number and I got no answer. I couldn't sleep all night. Finally, I called his father, my daughter, and my older son. Everybody tried to reach him, but to no avail. I was worried with all that was going on with young men. However, my spirit was good; it told me he was okay. Three a.m. came, and he put his key in the door. I said, "Come here! Where were you?" He lied, "You didn't come get me. I had to take the train. It took too long." "Yeah, right," I said. His father was on the phone. I gave the phone to my son. Finally, I could rest. I let the father handle that one. Distractions are designed for me to get me off my course. I was in the process of doing another production. My mind was overloaded and my soul was weary. In spite of it all, I had to go on. My next production, a play for women, was a concept my Pastor asked me to write, who is also, female. People don't realize that working with a group of people that you've never met is taxing. Also, trying to get them to catch the vision is exhausting mentally, physically, and spiritual. Often I would go home and cry. Not because of anything in particular, just from feeling drained. Then, I would have to get all prayed up for the next round. My God! With all due respect to all the cast members past and present, we eventually came on one accord. I know it was God that showed up every time, and for that I am truly grateful.

Besides the family, friends, and cast members, who had to endure my drama, so did MY HEAD! What was going on in there was a rollercoaster ride! I had to think of every aspect of production, how to be there wholeheartedly for my children, and how to put my acquaintances in their proper perspective. My mind was on overload! Often I had to retreat within myself to escape the realities of all my situations. In spite of it all, I had the grace of God to bring me through victoriously. For that, I am sincerely grateful.

CHAPTER 11

God's Grace

In the Bible, there are many scriptures about grace and mercy. But what do we really know about grace? I say it was when I walked out in the street and almost got hit by a car, by the skin of my teeth; or maybe when I went to New Orleans, two weeks before Hurricane Katrina. This was the timing of God's grace. Even when I went to Israel in May 2014 and in July, Israel was attacked in the very same places I had just left. I prayed that God keeps his protection over them. Grace is a funny thing though. The definition of grace is "the free and unmerited favor of God as manifested in salvation of sinners and the bestowal of blessings." There are different forms of Grace. Let's look at them. Let's start with:

Finding Grace

1. *Esther 2:16–17*, Do you remember the story about Esther who won grace and favor over all the other virgins, and was made Queen?

2. *Jeremiah 31:2–3*, The Lord said: "The people who survived the sword found Grace in the wilderness."

3. *Acts 15:39–40*, there was a disagreement between Barnabas and Paul, about what who to take so, they separated. Paul took Silas having been commended by the brothers to the Grace of the Lord.

4. *2 Corinthians: 12:8–9*, "…three times I pleaded with the Lord about this, that it should leave me. But He said to me 'My grace is sufficient for you, for my power is made perfect and weakness.' Therefore I will boast all the more gladly of my weaknesses so that the power of Christ may rest upon me."

5. *Hebrews 4:16*, "Let us then with confidence draw near to the throne of grace,

that we may receive mercy and find grace to help in time of need."

Powerful Grace

6. *John 1:14*, "And the Word became flesh and dwelt among us, and we have seen His glory, glory as the only son from the Father, full of grace and truth."
7. *Acts 4:33*, "And with great power the apostles were given their testimony to the resurrection of the Lord Jesus and great grace was upon them all."
8. *Acts 6:8*, "And Stephen full of grace and power were doing great wonders and signs among the people."
9. *Acts 11:22–24*, "The report of this came to the edge of the church in Jerusalem and they sent Barnabas to Antioch. When he came and saw the grace of God, he was glad, and he exhorted them all to remain faithful to the Lord with steadfast purpose, so he was a good man full of the Holy

Spirit in of faith. And a great many people were added to the Lord."

10. *Acts 14:1–3*, "Now at Iconium they entered together into the Jewish synagogue and spoke in such a way that a great number of both Jews and Greeks believed. But the unbelieving Jews stirred up the Gentiles and poisoned their minds against the brothers. So they remained for a long time, speaking boldly for the Lord, who bore witness to the word of his grace, granting signs and wonders to be done by their hands."

Receiving Grace

11. *John 1:15–17*, "(John bore witness about him and cried out this was he of whom I said 'He who comes after me ranks before me, because he was before me.') and from his fullness we have all received grace upon grace. For the law was given to Moses, grace and truth came through Jesus Christ."

12. *Acts 20:32*, "And now I commend you to God and to the word of his Grace, which is able to build you up and give you the inheritance among all those who are sanctified."

13. *Romans 1:1–5*, "Paul, a servant of Christ Jesus, called to be an Apostle, set apart for the Gospel of God, which he promised beforehand through his prophets in the Holy Scriptures, concerning his Son, who was descended from David according to the flesh and was declared to be the Son of God in power according to the Spirit of Holiness by resurrection from the dead, Jesus Christ our Lord, through whom we have received Grace and Apostleship to bring about the obedience of faith for the sake of his name among all nations."

14. *Hebrews 12:15*, "See to it that no one fails to obtain the Grace of God; that no 'root of bitterness' springs up and causes trouble, and by it many become defiled."

15. *1 Peter 5:10*, "And after you have suffered a little while, the God of all Grace, who has

called you to his eternal Glory in Christ, will himself restore, confirm, strengthen, and establish you."

Grace: A Gift Eternal

16. *Romans 3:20–24*, "for by works of the law no human being will be justified in his sight, since through the law comes knowledge of sin. But now righteousness of God has been manifested apart from the law, although the law and the Prophets bear witness to it-the righteousness of God through faith in Jesus Christ for all those who believe. For there is no distinction: for all have sinned and fall short of the glory of God, and are justified by his Grace as a gift, through the redemption that is in Christ Jesus."

17. *Romans 4:15–17*, "for the law brings wrath, but where there is no law there is no transgression. That is why it depends on faith, in order that the promise may rest

on Grace and be guaranteed to all his off-spring-not only to the adherent of the law but also to the one who shares the faith of Abraham, who is the father of us all, as it is written, 'I have made you the father of many nations' -in the presence of the God in whom he believed, who gives life to the dead and calls into existence the things that do not exist."

18. *Romans 5:1–2*, "Therefore, since we have been justified by faith, we have peace with God through our Lord Jesus Christ. Through him we have also obtained access by faith into this Grace in which we stand, and rejoice in hope of the Glory of God."

19. *Romans 5:12–21*, "Therefore, just as sin came into the world through one man, and death through sin, and so death spread to all men because all sinned-for sin indeed was in the world before the law was given, but sin is not counted where there is no law. Yet death reigned from Adam to Moses, even over those whose sinning

was not like you transgression of Adam, who was a type of one who was to come? But the free gift is not like the trespass. For if many died through one man's trespass, much more have the Grace of God and the free gift by the Grace of that one man Jesus Christ abound for many. And the free gift is not like the result of that one man's sin. For the judgment following one trespass brought condemnation, but the free gift following many trespasses brought justification." "For if, because of one man's trespass, death reigned through that one man's, much more will those who receive the abundance of Grace and the free gift of righteousness reign in life through the one man Jesus Christ. Therefore, as one trespass led to condemnation for all men, so one act of righteousness leads to justification and life for all men. For as by the one man's disobedience the many were made sinners, so by the one man's obedience the many will be righteous. Now the law came in to increase the trespass, but when sin increased Grace abounded all the more, so that, as sin reigned in death, Grace also might reign through righteousness leading to eternal life through Jesus Christ our Lord."

20. *Ephesians 2:4–9*, "But God, being rich in mercy, because of the Great Love with which he Loved us, even when we were dead in our trespasses, made us alive together with Christ- by Grace you have been saved-and raised us up with him and seated us with him in the heavenly places in Christ Jesus, so that in the coming ages he might show the immeasurable riches of his Grace in kindness toward us in Christ Jesus. For Grace has saved you through faith. And this is not your own doing; it is the gift of God, not a result of works, so that no one may boast."

So, there you have them, twenty scriptures on the grace of God. According to the Bible, you can find grace when you don't expect the unexpected and it happens anyway.

Powerful Grace: Like when I gave a neighbor a Bible because she was struggling with drugs nine years ago and her sister said: "She reads it every night with her Mom and hasn't used drugs since."

Receiving Grace: To be used by God to help others establish a relationship with our Lord Jesus Christ.

Grace: A Gift Eternal: When you have a terrible car accident and you escape with minor scrapes and bruises. What an awesome God we serve!

As you read through these scriptures, try and identify events in your life that relates to the different forms of grace. I know I receive grace every single day that I am alive. I thank the Lord every day for being here. I pray my biography inspires, enlightens, and encourages your life.

Summary

In closing, I pray *Weeding Out the Riffraff* will help propel forward all who read this book into a more fulfilling life, most importantly, establishing a relationship with the God to a place of understanding. As I wrote this book, I often reflected on all of the trials and tribulations I encountered. These experiences helped shape and mold me into the person I am today. Although it was very trying and depressing at times, I know that God was with me all of the way. If it had not been for the Lord on my side, where would I be?

The chapters I wrote about were very significant to my life. I could have escaped within myself, never to return to reality. I came close to losing my mind but a force greater than me would always step in and rescue me. I couldn't see, touch, or taste it, but I sure felt it. All of my uncertainties caused me to dream and believe I can make it. It was something in me that wouldn't allow me to go into directions that would destroy my entire life. So, again I say, my desire is to impact lives with my writing. I would like to take this time to thank all of you who read my memoirs. I pray you find your truths and share yours with the world, just as I did. We are here to help each other. May you be blessed beyond measure and go forth from here into the marvelous light! Here I am today. Looking and feeling great! God has truly saved me. I am a vessel for the Lord and I'm loving it. When you are able to help others, you know your call is great. I just want to run this race and look forward to that day when I hear God say, "Enter into the joy of the Lord, my Good and Faithful Servant." I know I have a long way to go, but I do believe I'm on the right pathway. My last words of encouragement: Change your perception and change your life. Be blessed and remember "Keep God First." Talk to him about everything especially your love life. Stay safe. God bless you!

A Note from the Editor

I have edited many manu-
scripts throughout my ca-
reer, but this life account
was one of my most en-
lightening   experiences
ever! As I was reviewing
Leslie's content, I saw
glimpses of my own life

experiences flash before my eyes and mind. As
I read and turned each page, I looked back and
saw the hell I had escaped, and it caused me to
appreciate the delivering power of God, on a
whole different level! I saw in Leslie's writings
the countless lives of many women, who *I know*
will be able to identify with the account of her
story and will clearly acknowledge the changes
that God has made for them, shouting as I did,
"Hallelujah, thank God for saving me!" I also

see the many lives of women yet to be touched, healed, delivered, and made whole, who are currently facing some of these same, exact situations. Oh, but when they read *Weeding Out the Riffraff*, in pursuit of their spiritual journey, they will know and be assured that there is hope and a way out for them, through Jesus, their Savior, Healer, and Deliverer. To God be the Glory!!!

This book is a must read *and* share. I encourage *everyone* who obtains a copy of this book to *automatically* purchase at least two, because there is *definitely* someone you know, who you need to help by giving them this book. Give them the gift of the saving knowledge of Jesus Christ an opportunity that will change their lives forever! Thank you, Leslie, for the privilege and honor of being a part of telling your life story. This is only the beginning…

La Verne Spruill

Spruill Business Services, LLC
732-900-1470

Made in the USA
Middletown, DE
26 April 2022

64798824R00077